# BLOODY CONTRACT

Keem-Holems Ojei

**Hambremen Ltd.**

Copyright © 2022 Keem-Holems Ojei

All rights reserved

The characters and events portrayed in this book are fictitious. Any similarity to real persons, living or dead, is coincidental and not intended by the author.

No part of this book may be reproduced, or stored in a retrieval system, or transmitted in any form or by any means, electronic, mechanical, photocopying, recording, or otherwise, without express written permission of the publisher.

ISBN: 9798815992993

*God is awesome.*

# CONTENTS

Title Page
Copyright
Dedication
Chapter 1 — 1
Chapter 2 — 13
Chapter 3 — 21
Chapter 4 — 33
Chapter 5 — 47
Chapter 6 — 61
Chapter 7 — 66
Chapter 8 — 73
The Last Chapter — 82
About The Author — 85

# CHAPTER 1

The helicopter landed on the open field, just ten yards ahead of me. The propeller distorted everything around with its powerful speed. One of the doors jerked open. They came one after the other. They were neatly dressed like businessmen: black suits on white shirts, blue ties, and black pairs of shoes. I saw them advancing towards me. I was scared. *Who're these people?* No matter what, I was ready to cooperate because I was lost in this jungle. This was quite a very lonely place where l found myself –and more so I needed help as fast as possible. When they got to the spot l was standing, one of them asked me, "Hello, what are you doing here all alone?"

"I got lost. I can't really explain. At the moment I am in a very bad state. Please l need your help."

"We're tourists from South Africa," he said. "My name is Greg. These are my colleagues – Jim and James. I want to assure you of your safety."

"Thank you very much. My name is Max," l said.

"Ok, please come with us," said Greg. He wore a clean

haircut.

The three men – of middle age- walked me into the chopper. I belted up at the back seat before the chopper lifted off from the ground. As the Chopper ascended into the sky, landscapes dropped off literally behind us. It was when I noticed the barrel of a shotgun behind where one of the men sat, that my blood froze for a while. I just realized how unsafe I was or thought to be. They were strangers – that was enough to scare me. Another thought of where they were probably flying me to was another issue to brainstorm on. But l was so scared and extremely uncomfortable not to ask any questions.

I looked down as we climbed up the sky, noticing the chirruping Robin birds as they flew angrily off the branches of trees. The image of crawling red-head lizards gaping into the sky crossed my mind's eyes.

We flew for about twenty minutes initially atop forests until I started noticing a network of interconnected roads, beautiful skyscrapers, well-cut roads, walkways, streets, lawns, well-trimmed flowers, and cars. After a while, the chopper began to lose altitude.

The chopper landed on a wide red circle inside a large compound in front of which was a large building.

The wholly white painted room was rectangular,

and approximately eight feet long and six-feet wide. The tiled ceiling was milk-colored. The floor bore white tiles. Only one door led to this room that bore no windows. Though it wasn't night, three fluorescent lights illuminated the room. I noticed some medical equipment and machines of various types, which I hadn't seen before in my life. There was a lone bed in the room dressed with a white sheet, and a chair stood by its side. On this bed, I lay, in green coverall. On my left, a white plastic container of drip was hung on a pole, and a slim, white plastic channel ran down from it to my left arm. For a while, I surveyed the place in wonderment. *"Oh my God! How did I get in here? Where am I? Another mystery!"*

The door creaked open and in came a lady. She was cute, dressed in white like a nurse. She gave me a toothy smile after shutting the door behind her, then walked toward the bed where I lay. She bent down and kissed my chin. "Don't worry too much, it will come to pass." Her voice was laced with a drawled, sweet British accent.
I forced my lips to part to speak to her, to actually test if I could now speak!

"Where am I, oh, dear nurse?"

"Relax. You are exhausted."

"Who are you and where am I? But why the drip? How did I get here?"

"I'm a nurse in this private clinic. We're going to carry out an X-ray on your brain. The drip is a necessity," she said. "You're very weak, from the various tests we ran on you."

"Holy Moses!" I said in deep pain. "What X-ray?"

"A brain MRT X-ray. Simply put, MRT is a Magnetic Resonance Tomography…to examine your brain.` `

"Is there something wrong with your brain?" I asked her sarcastically.
After a short while, a thickset, middle-aged man walked in and closed the door behind him. He was carrying a plastic tray containing bottled water, sandwiches, and sliced tomato. The nurse took the tray from the man and he walked away immediately.

"Now, sit up and eat," she said.

I placed the second pillow on top of the first and adjusted myself. I took the tray and started eating. She left the room. A h*ungry man,* I thought aloud, *is an angry man…*

Time passed. The nurse came in again when the drip was almost running out.
"Now tell me how I got here and ….."

"Not now, dear. You're exhausted now. Relax, please. You were actually in a coma when you were brought here. You need some rest –much of it – ok." He studied my face and said, "You're such a handsome young man."

"Thank you," I said. "But that is not my major concern now."

"The doctor will see you any moment from now," she added.
Shortly after, a young, nice-looking doctor stepped in. He was a beefy, good-looking,
Average-height white man, dressed in white trousers and white overcoat, hanging a stethoscope on his shoulders.
He removed the drip and ordered the nurse who came in with him to fetch a glass of milk.

"Doctor, why am l here."

"You are our patient. Some men brought you here for treatment…for general examination and treatment…. that's what we're doing," the doctor replied. "Does that answer your question?"

"Doctor, I don't even know them from Adam. They picked me up from somewhere, put me in their helicopter…and that was all I knew…" I tried to explain, but he interrupted me.

"They'll be here soon, but they left one of them to watch over you. Ask all your questions when they come back, okay." He stepped out, leaving the two nurses behind.

I slept off about half an hour later. When the friendly nurse woke me up the next day, she told me the time was 11:00 A.M. I guessed I must have slept for a very long time.
She smiled and said, "Looks like you're okay now. You look lovely this morning." Was she teasing me?

"I forgot to ask your name yesterday. What's your name?" I asked.

She didn't hesitate to give me her name. "Rita Shores."

"What a lovely name!"

"Thank you."

"So, what's really going on here, Rita?"

"I don't really understand, dear. An armed man has been on guard since you were brought in here?"

"What for then? For me?" I asked with a mournful smile on my chin.

"I don't know. That could probably be for your security," she said.
They might be thinking that you could escape. You're worth gold to them as it now seems."

Rita was not ready to answer any further questions. She left the scene.

Ten minutes later, four men came into the room with the doctor. I heard him tell them that I would be alright soon.

"Hope you're doing better today?" asked one of them.

"Yes, thank you."

They surveyed me and went away immediately. I could remember who they were: they were the men that flew me on the helicopter. I remember how scared I was when they ordered me into the helicopter.

On the fourth day, I felt I was seriously having a secret crush on the nurse Rita. She was very nice and caring to me.

Deep down in my heart, I was very much scared of these strangers that brought me here on their helicopter. *What is their plan*? I kept thinking. On second thought it was amazing to me how help came to me from the strange wandering in the forest where I got lost. It was a forest of mysteries, a forest where 1 witnessed mystifying activities. These people saved me by picking me up to where they did. Who were they looking for when they spotted me? Was this God's work? My confused thoughts were making me clinically nervous – that would not be an overstatement. I picked up a recent magazine on the magazine rack at the reception and started browsing through it.

For the second time, the thought of escape came to my mind and I wrestled over it.

As I was thumbing through the pages of the newspaper I picked up in the room, someone caressingly touched my neck from my back. I turned around, and behold, it was Rita. Was she in love too? I could sense some spark of love. I smiled. She smiled back in reciprocation as she came forward and leaned on me, at the same time kissing me on my left cheek. I felt a sudden hardness of my organ. She looked into my eyes and gave me a hard smile. Her hair had been properly coiffured and smelled of some kind of freshness. I also noticed that she was wearing a slight, but distinctly made face make-up.

I said with a smile, "I hope you don't wear Brazilian hair. It's in vogue with ladies these days."

She laughed out hilariously. "No, sir, I wear my natural hair. Why do you ask?"

"Your natural hair is long and beautiful, my dear."

"Thanks. In a few days from now, you'll be leaving me, right?" she said bitterly. There was somewhat potential anxiety in her eyes when she made that remark that gave me the impression that she was also in love with me.

Her head was bent to the left and she probably forgot

to dim her eyes, as her lower lip dropped slightly and indistinctly. I knew she only expressed her feelings.

"So, you would wish I remained in this clinic with you?" I just realized that my remark was not polite enough for her assimilation.

"You were not meant to remain here, certainly…only that you were brought here for some very special reason."

I brilliantly changed the topic of discussion. "When are those men coming back here?"

"Probably on Friday," she said.

I reached forward and placed my hand on her lap. She was indifferent. "Is there any way I can escape from here?" I made that remark indifferently, in a very low tone.

I sensed her giving a resignation of ideas as she tilted her head to the left, stared at me sternly, and remained quiet for a while. She returned her hard gaze at me after a while and said, in a whisper, "It won't work out at all. I don't think it will work. It'd be like handling a life bomb. I told you earlier that there is an armed guard out there. They've been working on shifts since you were brought in here."

"That means these guys are in for real business." If I was shocked, I didn't show it this time. "That means there's no means of escape?"

At this point in time, I decided to give up the idea of ever escaping. Cooperating with these strange gangsters was the option left to remain alive. I raised my head to speak. She looked up at me and I discovered an unfamiliar expression on her face. "Well, I've made up my mind to 'give in'. Whatever it is, I'm in," I said, getting deeper in thought.

She looked down and continued to tap her right foot on the tiled floor. After a while, she walked out and shut the door behind her. I looked out through the window and saw the setting sun. The elliptical ball of the sun was glowing and appeared really pregnant.

I went into the reception room and picked up another magazine, this time, *Ebony*.
A few minutes later, Rita saw me at the reception and walked towards me. I looked into her face. She smiled unimaginatively. "Have those guys settled the bill?" I asked politely.

"Why? The payment has nothing to do with me either," said Rita politely. "But I think the doctor must have struck a good deal with them...whatever; l can't say." After a deep thought, she retreated: "I don't know why I've been relating so well with you. These are official secrets, as it were. Right from the time l set my eyes on you, I've not been myself. I've met many patients in this clinic...but can't explain that with your case. Should I call you the magic man? You've swept me off my feet."

I smiled. Her expressions gladdened my heart. There was a short silence.

She continued, "I don't want us to lose contact. Wherever you may be, try and keep in touch, please. I want to see you again, honey."

"Where do you live?" I asked.

She took out a jotter and wrote her telephone number and address without any hesitation. She left shortly to answer a phone call. When she came back, she told me the doctor wanted to see me.

"We're through with you now. You have to go with them. You've been Certified okay" The doctor concluded.

*You've been certified okay:* That statement sank into my brain like a pang.

A Cadillac convertible was parked at the nylon-tarred drive. Two stern-looking men, armed with automatic shotguns, were leaning on a black Range Rover SUV that was parked behind the Cadillac.

I was asked to get into the back seat of the Range Rover. The two SUVs drove smoothly down the long drive, then onto the highway.

The evening was windy and at seven degrees, it was

chilly. I couldn't fathom where we were headed!

# CHAPTER 2

The two wonders-on-wheel sped smoothly down the light traffic. The man sitting close to me spoke for the first time as the car stopped at the traffic light. "Let me introduce myself the second time: I'm called Gregory Hill, Greg for short, and these are my men. I cut the shots here. But you're going to work with only two of them, as the occasion warrants. You've been confirmed okay for the 'contract' at hand. So, you're now our partner. When you cooperate with us, we cooperate with you. You've got to play the game intelligently," he concluded. The traffic light changed from red to amber and then green. "The 'contract' is a complicated one. But it needs brain and tact." My lower lip sagged when he made that last statement. All the while, I listened intently. "We had kidnapped two Americans to do the job, but their medical history was unsuitable." He paused again and brought out a packet of cigars. He opened it, slid one stick out, and pushed it between his teeth. He offered the packet to me."

"Thank you, sir. I don't smoke." I still decided not to ask what the contract was. I decided to keep calm and play along. He brought out a lighter and lighted the fat cigar and wound down the side of his window slightly.

"You see, we were in search of important stuff above that thick bush when we spotted you. We felt you were stranded and needed help. Nobody goes picnicking in that kind of thick forest all alone."

"I'm listening, sir," I said.

He blew smoke through the window of the car, fingered his tie, hand-combed his mustache, and straightened up. "That's just that. We got a piece of advice from an intellectual psychologist to try and get a suitable and capable person to do the job." There was a short silence. "You will be making yourself some million bucks if the 'contract' becomes successful. You'll be provided with all you'd need: a car, a fine apartment, enough dollars; and you have to work out the necessary clues. Do you know why the doctor tested your brain with those hi-tech machines?"

I shook my head. "No, sir," I answered.

"To see if you are clairvoyant; to see if you can take facts from people you've never met before: picking on people's brain at first blush; if you are eligible to the holding of top secrets. How about that?"

I shook my head in bewilderment.

"Gentleman," he said as he turned and faced me,

puffing smoke in my direction. Hell! I clipped my nose with my fingers. "We're putting you in a hotel for the meantime. I want to tell you my last word, my young friend." Now…" he squeezed his face cruelly in the form of a threat. "Dare you not try and escape, for we are keeping a close tab on you."

That left a grotesque fear in me. After a long drive, the two cars came to a halt in front of a long barrier. The barrier was lifted up electronically and drove the Cadillac and the Land Rover. Both drivers were offered small red rectangular cards each. An imposing skyscraper was right in front of us as we drove into the compound. It posed like a hotel building from all indications. It was a thirty-floor block. There were beautifully trimmed funnel-like flowers arranged in rows. The parking lot, by my estimation, could accommodate at least thirty exotic cars.

Both cars were parked in two vacant parking bays, in between a Rolls Royce and a Datsun Sunny. We stepped down and walked past the revolving doors into the well-decorated reception lobby at one end of the hall. There was a sprawl of cane-chairs, settees, and arm-chairs. The floor was brilliantly titled. There were a number of mercury bulbs shining and making the room very captivating. At strategic points were placed potted indoor flowers in the class of Begonia, Carnation, Dahlia, and Forsythia.

We joined two other men sitting on two settees. We

had handshakes and sat down with them. Gregory ordered some drinks, sandwiches and fried turkey. I decided to feed my eyes on the beauty of the lobby bar and the sculptural designs, et al.

Few minutes after we were well seated, Gregory Hills broke the ice: "We're private detectives and I'm the Managing Partner of Huge Dogs Inc., Philadelphia. We're very organized." He dropped the last dwarf of the cigar in an ashtray placed on the small chair-side table. He looked up and pointed his finger. "That's Inspector Jim Harley," Harley was short, stocky, and looked like someone who could fight with a bull. "And the tall young man is Detective Inspector James Coins."

The waiter came with a well-designed tray on which were placed glasses of wine and some sandwiches. The waiter lowered the tray and when he came towards me, I stretched out my hand and took one glass of wine and a sandwich. I stole a quick, wicked glance at Gregory and saw him sipping on his wine. I sipped on my wine and was quiet for a long while. He resumed his speech shortly after. He looked at me and said, "Jim Harley and James Coins would be working with you for the time being."

I nodded. They all could observe the anger on my face. It was no longer hidden. I was still anxious to be acquainted with the so-called contract that they need me to deliver. I was fighting with so many questions in my brain. I had to let it out now. I ran out of patience and asked him for the first time, "Mr. Greg, kindly let me know what the deal, the contract is all about, sir."

"I'll tell you very soon," he said.

James Coins poured more drinks for all. He ordered more Cognac and a full pack of roasted stick meat. Greg Hills stood up for the first time. He was completely bald or he was used to skin-cut. He wore an aristocratic nose - to my admiration. He was slim, tall, and should be in his mid-fifties. I saw him walk to the front desk and seemed to be negotiating with the porter there. Five minutes later he walked back to his settee clutching a plasticized card key and an attached small red rectangular strap tagged 'RM. 476.' I examined it well after he gave it to me.

"Let's all check out the room," said Gregory Hills. I stood up and noticed the other gentlemen climb onto their feet. Greg led the way. We walked past collected numbers of people having some drinks and snacks. I noticed a well-dressed young man in a suit and black tie pacing to and fro the corridor. I guessed he could be a security man.

Four of us rode the elevator to the 4$^{th}$ floor. We marched out of the elevator when we got to the 4$^{th}$ floor and then walked down the dimly-lit, resplendent, and parallel corridor, searching for 476. The floor bore very well polished tiles, lined on both sides with potted chrysanthemum flowers.

When we got to the doorstep, Gregory signaled me to open the door, which l did.
My eyes wandered around the room instantaneously. The room was rectangular and moderately large. The floor bore green tiles which appeared recently polished. As I was admiring the room, the room service arrived with the necessary toiletries meant for the room. I walked toward the window and parted the blinds. I noticed an Olympic-sized blue swimming pool in the courtyard down below. The double-decker bed was well dressed in a pure-white sheet and it bore six pillows. I noticed a grey telephone placed on a small stool just at the head end of the bed. There was a desk and an upright chair placed at my left-hand side. The large, smart television was placed against the wall.
For the first time, I noticed a door leading into another room. I guessed it led to the bath.
"How do you like your room?" asked Greg Hills. He appeared quite intelligent and Eagle-eyed and spoke like one of those men with high IQ, from his use of language and the way he carried himself. The room service man left and shut the door behind him.

"I love it," I replied.

"So, you'll be working from here till further notice. Now, we can talk," he said. They all came closer and he spoke in a low tone, pausing in the process. "We want to bring one New York City-based multi-millionaire singer to our custody. He's a fast-growing artist in the musical field and a fast-growing artist at that. He has had about five singles and he's turning the world around. Though those releases are profound, someone is not happy about it …somebody somewhere. For the past nine months, he's sold over ten million albums." He paused briefly, took a stern look into my face, and noticed that it was changing color. He resumed his speech. "The name of this famous artist is Jerry Martins. J-Martins. The name rings a bell, right? He could be your fan! But business is business. You're going to make yourself some bucks."

''You mean, to kidnap him?'' I asked with so much curiosity.

''Something of that nature,'' said James Coins.

''But I've never done such a thing in my life, sir.''

''That's not an issue. That's why you will be working with James Coins and Jim Harley. They're going to train you, and you'll be fine, ok," Gregory Hills tried to convince me. But I was wondering….*Why me…?*

''Who wants J-Martins kidnapped?'' was my first

determinant question.

"You'll receive a further briefing, Max," Greg concluded.

They noticed the change in my countenance and my head tilting gradually towards my left shoulder was a somewhat warning to them that this news (or contract as they named it) had demoralized me. They heard me take a long, deep breath. For the third time in a few days, l was confused. I drew in a deeper breath. I discovered I had no alternative but to take the bulls by the horns. Should I call the police? This thought hung on for a while. I recalled what Gregory Hills told me earlier: *``Dare you not try to escape, because we're watching your back....*"Your share is five million United States dollars. How would you like a two-week-long vacation with your spouse in the Bahamas after the contract?" said Gregory. I tried to concur when I heard the amount, but it didn't flow. My mind was clouded with so many questions. "Your pseudonym for this operation is Dick," Greg seemed to conclude.

I took up the cudgels. There was seemingly a sword of Damocles hanging over my head.

# CHAPTER 3

Jim Harley and James Coins walked me through a short course that lasted about one month: it was more on intelligence, sprinting, military/martial arts maneuver drills. I had to also get acquainted with the streets and environment where J-Martins' residence was situated for proper 24-hour surveillance. The duo also taught me the best way to handle and use all sorts of weapons. The martial art drill was the most eventful. I learned so fast.

Amongst other items that were provided for me after the training were a fairly used (six-year-old) Buick Century automobile and a special revolver shotgun. I eventually made up my personal, clandestine plans – to hire some young girls who could help me gather intelligence on the 'contract' at hand.

Moreover, I had been given half a million bucks, being part payment for the contract. I was already planning in my mind's eyes, how l was going to spend the whopping sum of USD$5m. Five million bucks could literally buy half of the properties in Los Angeles!

I climbed out of the bed and prayed shortly. I took a

long shower afterward. I was dressing up when my telephone rang.

"Good morning."

"Hello," said a familiar voice. It was the voice of Gregory Hills. "How are you fairing, Dick?" Dick was a decoy name for the operation, or the contract rather.

"Everything is moving as planned, sir."

"I learned you've just completed the drills yesterday, and you're going into operation today."
"Don't think we have our fingers folded. "We're gathering info and monitoring the entire organigram and knowing when to tell you to strike…and also watching your back too."

"That's in order, sir."

"We talk later in the day," he said and dropped the phone.

Half an hour later, I rode the elevator to the hotel lobby. The hotel bar was filled with people of mixed colors. I walked past the revolving door, stepped onto the short walkway, and trotted towards my car parked on Bay 27. I got into the Buick convertible, started the engine, and drove off almost immediately. It was Sunday and I was meant to find Rita Shores' residence. I drove at an average speed, following the sometimes funny directions by the invisible young lady in the Navigator – in hundred meters, turn left; in fifty meters turn right; make a U-turn; make the next turn in five hundred meters, etc.

Twenty minutes' drive brought me to the beautiful Palm Avenue. It was palm fronds-lined and quite a quiet street to drive through. No. 10 Luncheon Avenue was just by the corner. "In ten meters you have come to your final destination," announced the young voice on the navigator. On a smart, quick glance at my rearview mirror, I noticed for the third time a particular car tailing me. Who could they be - Jim and James?

I parked the car just on a vacant bay, came down, shut the door, and walked towards the portico of the beautiful building. I dialed her number and told Rita l was right at her residence. She was happy to hear my voice.

I walked up the stairs to the second floor as she instructed. An oak-paneled French door carved on it by the sculptor of Martin Luther King (Jr.) was the door of the entrance to her apartment. The entire vicinity was as quiet as a mouse's resting place. I was not surprised when l saw the queen as she tucked her head through the door to confirm who the visitor was. Her bright warm eyes were romantic in such a way that I felt like starting a 'kissing course' right from the door. Her soft small lips, softly coiffured hair, and smile got me disarmed at first! As she appeared, I saw her beautiful fingers crawling up my shoulders and her lips staining mine with lipstick as I walked just one step forward. She probably read my mind! Jeezzz.

"Oh...happy to see you, Max. You're welcome. I really missed you!" The softness of her voice, in combination with her eloquence, was so charismatic and something to behold. My heartbeat felt some elation. *Was this the Rita I met at the Philadelphia hospital that nursed me? But she didn't then show me that she was in love!*
We walked inside the living room and she shut the door. We held ourselves tight for close to three minutes, kissing and caressing each other passionately. Her tongue slipped into my mouth, on top of my tongue... systematically.... and I gripped the opportunity as graciously as l could as though today was the end of the world..... She was in her dressing gown. The feminine approach to the softness of her bulk body (pointed breasts and sprawled pair of bottom) got me confused. It was as though she was prepared to 'take me' from the door when I arrived. Ha! Women are powerful! Rita was a very beautiful black American qualified nurse. Her aristocratic nose and her shape had been my admiration. Her mental uprightness and brilliance had also made me fall in love with her. She was a good woman with a very good heart. I have done my research: all men all over the world love women with a good heart. No man likes a nagging

woman. My right hand wandered down towards her beautiful laps. I noticed that the speed of her breathing and heart suddenly changed gear. As I crawled my fingers down to her buttocks, she held my fingers and said, "What do you want to do?"

"Nothing." My chest pressed down on her fine pointed breasts which were now very stiff.

"Tell me what you want to do, Max."

"I want to do it. You've charged me up," I said.

"I can't do it now. I'm not free. Next time; we'll just know ourselves."

I softly eased myself from her. "You're crazy. You've taken me to the sky and now this?"

"Really? You can't be serious," she said, laughing. "You better come down from the sky…"

I sat down. She left the lounging room, swaying her hips deliberately for me to notice how large and well-shaped her bottom was. I smiled. *Women!!* As she stepped out l took out time to eye-survey the luxuriously furnished apartment. There were red-colored leather settees, arm-chairs, and a glass center table. The lounging chairs overlooked the wall divider cabinet. The room bore decorations of some artistic carvings, a magazine rack, and potted indoor flowers. A cute place.

She came back re-dressed and had with her a tray of orange juice, ice, and a bottle of red wine. She was now in jeans trousers and a red, round-neck, sleeveless shirt.
She came towards me still swaying her hips. She sat across my legs and held me by my shoulders. "Serve yourself."

"You seem to be off-duty today?" I asked her, looking directly into her eyes.

"I've resigned. It's a dirty job," she said.

"Say that again. Dirty job, nursing? In-vogue job it is. Men and women are trooping into the profession these days. "Were you fired?"

"No."

"You want to venture into business?"

"Yes, business. I've got my own company long before I resigned. It's now six months old. I want to give it full attention."

"What business are we talking about here?"

"Klassique Salon: manicure, pedicure, hair styling, haircut, massage for both sexes, makeup and tattoo studio; it's not very far from here. I started it big. It's a three-floor block…..the business occupies the entire block."

"That's a nice one. And I expect that's gonna be much more profitable."

"O yeah, you got it," she affirmed and grinned.

"What's your staff strength?"

"Twelve for now," said Rita.
"Who financed all these?"

"My mum."

"Your mum must be rich," I said with excitement.

"Yeah. You want to know everything…not too fast, nigger."

I opened the bottle of red wine and poured some in the two glass cups provided and gave her one glass. ''Toast. Chess.''

"Chess. So what's the contract…racket all about? You must've got all the hints now. Haven't you?"

"It's a tough one. I don't want to even think about it. A tough one indeed." She noticed my face got hardened. "It's about the kidnapping of a socialite. A popular one at that. I shouldn't be saying this…..l hope I can trust you."

She was visibly shocked by her reaction. I noticed her eyebrows opened up wider and her head jerked forward. "Who could that be, Maxx?"

"J-M…..Jerry Martins."

"Jerry Martins!?" She blew her top. She stood up from my laps, sat on the next armchair, and held her left hand akimbo, staring into my face. "Who wants him skimped?"

"That, I don't know, Rita."

"Jerry Martins is a young artist. He is a good singer." There was a short silence, punctuated by the sound of Teddy Pendergrass' music from an inner room's CD player. "Have you been paid for the job?"

"Some percentage."

"How are you now going about it? Don't forget these guys are watching your back," said Rita sarcastically.

"I feel like running away. I want to run away. Am not comfortable with this contract."
"Don't even try that bullshit. You're under their net, their surveillance. They might kill you. Don't forget they would've killed you if they wanted to, remembering the spot where they picked you from. Play along in the meantime. It's very dangerous to escape now. They will get you and kill you. Know that J-Martins have many bodyguards. How are you gonna succeed with this operation?"

"Look Rita dear, I am tied to some conditions. Those guys have my wallet. This wallet was given to me by a strange woman that I met in that forest. The old woman told me it contains a lot of wealth, which I should not give to anyone. After speaking to me the old woman had disappeared into thin air, to my amazement. Above all, Gregory Hills, the leader of the team, had warned me the umpteenth time that they are watching my back and listening to all my phone conversations."

She nodded. "This 'spiritual wallet' of yours could be the money you're going to make from the operation, l presume." Rita smiled.

"This hard way?"

"Well, you can never tell, my dear friend. Some money-making avenues are packaged in mysteries. It doesn't come easy. But I'll advise you to be very, very careful. Any mistake, you end up all your life in jail." I shook my head several times to register my confusion. She left and came back shortly with a tray. On the tray were two teacups brimming with hot coffee and two packets of crackers. "I want to see how l could assist."

"That would be a nice idea!" There was a brief silence as we watched some programs on the television. "You're really living in paradise here. A cute apartment you've got."

"I'll be going out soon, probably with you. I want to buy a Ford truck. Am changing my car. The Buick

I've been driving was inherited from my mum and it's old. I'm going to put it on sale. It's there in the garage." She stood up and went into a room through a door.

I stood up and started pacing up around the room. She appeared three minutes later wearing a black jacket and clutching a red handbag that matched the color of her high-heel shoes. We left the house and she opted to use my car. "You pay me 2 grand if we must use my car," I joked. She laughed louder than I expected. She was quite elated. We got into the car and drove down the lonely driveway. "So, which direction, my boss?"

"I suggest we should drive downtown," she said. "That's the place to purchase it at a much lower price."

"There's always a price tag," I affirmed. I turned on the music set and slot in the CD of Michael Bolton.

There were different brands of automobiles in their modernity, adjacent to each other. We met the well-dressed, smart-looking white American salesman whom we told we wanted to buy a Ford truck.

"You're welcome. My name is Austin Carter. Ford cars are very good products….don't mind the price. They're very durable, but we've got good prices for you," said the handsome salesman wearing a black suit with a white shirt and red tie. He had very strong charm and sex appeal that l noticed almost swept Rita off her feet. He conducted us around to have a good look at the various brands of cars. She also considered getting a different brand, apart from the Ford Lariat truck.

Rita finally settled for a Cadillac Escalade SUV. The salesman, Carter, took us to his cozy office and sat us down, left, and came back with two cups of coffee and cookies for Rita and me. "The cute SUV is only USD$49,020."

''What discount are you giving us," I asked Mr. Carter.

''It's discounted already - 6.5 percent discount on all our brands," he replied.
''Method of payment?" asked Rita.

''You make 25 percent down payment, the rest 75 percent on monthly direct payments from your bank account, until liquidation," Austin Carter responded politely.

''Perfect," Rita responded.

''The car is comfortable with a very cozy interior, automatic transmission….in fact, full option and fully loaded. You'll call me after one month to tell me how unique it's driving it."

"Great!" she said. ''When are we taking delivery?" Rita sneezed. She leaned forward and whispered into my ears. I nodded. In a short while, all the paper work was done before she brought out her checkbook, tore out a sheet, and filled the dotted spaces with her black pen.

"Your check will clear in a day or two at most. Before then, our engineers will do what is called a PDI (Pre-delivery Inspection) on the car. We will deliver the car for you at home….you give us your time from 14.00 hours. Thank you so much for your patronage sir, madam…We do hope you will send your friends to us if you're satisfied with our patronage."

# CHAPTER 4

I changed my hotel to a more local one in the heart of Manhattan, New York. I just had to do that because it would aid my better positioning of Jerry Martins' residence. I needed to study the environment very well, before intruding like a business tourist who had a strong entrepreneurial taste in music. I woke up this morning feeling very hungry and tipsy from the drinking spree of last night's outing with some friends. I finished half a bottle of VAT 69, blending occasionally with coca-cola and a dozen of ice. I had run into a former schoolmate of mine. He felt happy seeing me and wanted to know what I was doing in New York. "I'm on business, I'm looking for money, my guy. 'Want to be rich," I had told him. We were also able to hook on two cute ladies to hang out with us. At the end of the drinking spree, Ted took his girl home and I took mine to my hotel. She left my hotel room just before dawn because she said she needed to get to work early. She needed an hour's drive to get to work.

It was barely a couple of hours later that I heard two soft raps on my door. "Room service," I heard a voice say. She opened the door and came in. She was dressed in a blue uniform. She rolled in a small trolley that contained a tray on which were tea items, three slices of bread, half a chicken, and fried sausage on a plate. I remember placing that order before going to bed last night, against breakfast today.

"Good morning, sir," she said, smiling. "Is there any other thing you need sir?"

"Not really, thank you." She left the room shortly after. I rushed my breakfast. I was having the last sip of my coffee when the telephone rang. I picked up the receiver. "Hello?"

A familiar voice came on the line, but the telephone number of the caller was not displayed. "Hello Max…how are you doing? This is Hills. Please meet me before noon. It's very urgent."

"I hope everything is ok, sir?"

"Everything is ok. Leave your car, take an express train to Philadelphia city." He spoke further briefly in coded words –which Jim and James had already taught me. "See you soon." The telephone went dead at the other end.

I left my hotel in a chartered taxi to the express train station, early enough to catch the 8.30 A.M. train. I had under my holster, concealed by my black jacket, my powerful revolver shotgun. I bought a return ticket to Philadelphia.

A few hours later, I arrived in Philadelphia, Pennsylvania. I took a taxi to 78 Munro Avenue, as Gregory Hills directed. "When you get there, call me. A green painted Buick truck will be waiting to pick you up. The name of the man on the wheels is Jacob." When the taxi dropped me at the right spot, I noticed a green Buick parked along the road. I paid for the Uber taxi and walked to the Buick truck. The man at the wheels, on noticing me, surveyed me before he pulled down the catch of the door lock and signaled me to get in. The only word he uttered was, "What's my name?"

I smiled. "You're Jacob, I presume?"

"Thank you. You're Max?"

"Yes."

"Good to see you." The engine of the car was already running. He suddenly drove off with the screech of tortured tires towards an unknown direction. I sat calmly in the car. Jacob was not ready for any conversation. He was probably trained to act the way he was acting. After about twenty minutes' drive, he drove into a compound and asked to get down and pointed towards an oak-paneled door. "There's a man there, he'll tell you what to do, Max. See you soon."

I jumped down from the car and walked down the short portico towards a red oak door. The man l met there conducted me into a large sitting room via a corridor. He rapped, opened the door, looked in, called my name, came out, waved me on, and closed the door behind him.

I was shocked at the sight of the men I saw. They were all sitting on armchairs and settees, smoking fat cigars and drinking diluted whisky-on-the-rocks. The room was stuffed with smoke and the hell of the smell irritated me. They all smiled and shrugged as l advanced into the room. I quickly noticed Gregory Hills, Whit Brown, Humphrey Price, Jim Harley, and James Twins. They all wore black suits on white shirts. They were all staff of Gregory who operated the private detective firm - architects of the audacious 'Bloody-Contract.' I gave them a uniform salute as l noticed Gregory ushering me to a chair. Jim Harley said I should help myself to some cigars and whiskey. I filled a glass with Hennessy and tossed two ice cubes into it.

"You're a bit late, Max. Proper planning is on top gear," said Greg. "Jerry Martins' having a concert at Chamberlain Arts Square. He'll be arriving at 17.00 hours." He glanced at his wristwatch. I gulped down my drink and refilled it, adding three more ice cubes. Gregory Hills relaxed well in his armchair and continued to speak: 'The Chamberlain Arts Square (The-CAS) is a large theater downtown. It could seat up to ten thousand people. All tickets are sold out as l talk to you. This is record-breaking. But anyway, I've paid for six front seats, at the rate of $50 each. The front seat would give us a full-frontal view of the stage." He lit another cigar. "The job is not going to be that easy. J-Martins has about a dozen bodyguards." High-Grade Detective Gregory Hills continued shortly after lighting another cigar. "He'll be arriving in a motorcade and he'll be in the white Rolls Royce. After an hour in the show, you move to the parking lot, wearing your sunglasses and cigarette in hand. At the entrance gate, gently and indifferently walk to the Rolls Royce, put your right hand in your hip pocket, pretend as if you're getting out a packet of cigarettes. Allow the packet of cigarettes to fall near the wheel of the car of the Rolls. As you bend to pick it up, you slide this object very close to the tire, picking your packet of cigarette in the process." He handed me a small, sharp object. "Walk round to the chauffeur who will probably be sitting in the driver's seat or hanging around and ignite a tete-a-tete with him. "This object would definitely puncture the tires", he continued, "as soon as they want to drive off after the concert."

"Greg, be reminded that Rolls Royce cars are

specially built machines. The tires are very special. It can run on punctured tires for miles," said Humphrey.

"What I just handed to Max is a special one. I got it from Poland, on my last trip," continued Gregory. "As I was saying, since Martins wouldn't want to wait for the tires to be replaced, he may swap cars – he's impatient when it comes to something of this nature. And worst of all I've learnt that he doesn't like to ride in any other car than Rolls when he comes to concerts. Juan de Vicenti has provided us with his Rolls Royce. We are going with it. It will be parked very close to J-Martins'. It has been branded – Bella Services Rental. That would be loud enough to mean that it would be available to be rented. J-M might inquire for the services of Bella S. R. Maxx would be around, ready to do his marketing… etcetera, etcetera." James stood up and started pacing the hall, glass in hand, cigar in-between lips. He seemed to be either nervous or uncomfortable.

I glanced at the clock on the mantelpiece - it was exactly 16:06 hours."

The conversation cum plans went on for another half an hour, after which G-Hills stood up, took the last gulp from his drink, and disappeared into an inner room. He returned shortly with a red carton. He opened it and brought out two brand new shotgun revolvers and a very small bottle that looked like a bottle of perfume. That small bottle of perfume was the 'contract scent' – that was supposed to do the job on the TARGET, for the Contract to be successful! Jim and James were highly experienced, but retired, police officers. From the grapevines, they were fired from the police force because of the illegal engagements they were involved in. Presently, in furtherance to their livelihoods, they were stretching their activities into *'private contracts.'*

Shortly after, we all walked to the carport and got into the cars. I was asked to join Jim Harley and James Coin in the Land Rover. James was on the wheels.

We took a twenty-minute brisk drive to Chamberlain Volts square. The concert was just starting. The parking bays were filled up with a number of exotic cars. Among these cars, one particular one caught my attention – a luxurious white Rolls Royce, with two well-built men who seemed to look like bodyguards, leaning on it. That was his car! We parked our Rolls on the vacant bay closer to the white Rolls.

The American Jerry Martins was already on stage. He was about five foot eleven, slim, and quite handsome. From my research about him, he was of Cuban descent. He was marvelously dressed in a slim-fitting gold-colored sleeveless shirt and black glittering leather trousers. Adorned around his neck was a bunch of golden chains that would suggestively have cost him at least $50,000.

The stadium-sized theater was fully packed. J-Martins was the jovial type, as he occasionally made jokes to relax the spectators, making them laugh hilariously. The spectators were more of young ladies, who were clapping their hands with enthusiasm and trying to surge forward to touch his pants.

Deep in my heart, I began to feel sorry for him. Why would somebody somewhere have such a bad notion about another person to harm him....because of mere envy, money, and power? Anyways, five million dollars was a hell of bucks. I would be able to buy a property in San Francisco or San Diego at the end of the operation, codenamed *'Bloody Contract'*, l thought. But I foresaw a hard task ahead! Another mind told me to run away and inform the police and also risk being killed by these crooks if l get caught before getting to the police, because it would be tantamount to betrayal, in their book of records. They had made me swear an oath of secrecy. Time crawled on.

I left my seat. James and the gang noticed my moves. They nodded in apprehension. On my way out, I bought a sunshade, a full pack of yogurt and a packet of cigarettes from a small adjoining kiosk attached to the entrance 'C' wing of the theater block. Fifty yards behind me, towards the foot of the parking bay, I heard a voice. "Stop there, gentleman!" I froze but took brisk control of the emotion as fast as possible. I turned slowly like a robot and l was quick to notice an armed uniformed cop. He was a white American police sergeant; he wore a thin, thick-set face.

"Young man, where are you headed?" He was walking slowly towards me.

I smiled and greeted him. "Why do you ask? Isn't here a public place, or not? My Rolls is parked over there. What's the heck?"

"'I'm doing my job," he said.

As he approached me, I asked him, "Do you smoke?"

"Yes, but not when 'am on duty." As he approached me I hoisted a full packet of sealed cigarettes and tossed it towards him as he approached. He took it from me and said, "Thank you. But this will not avoid any arrest if you are found wanting." I smiled, but he didn't. He was having a .45 police special tucked into the holster beneath his belt position. I left him there and walked on. I turned after twenty yards and saw him lighting up a stick of one of the cigarettes. I smiled – he just told me he never smoked on duty! I walked on. As I approached Jerry Martins' Rolls Royce I turned again and looked back, then discovered that he was walking in the opposite direction. I plugged my left hand into my left pocket, brought out the pocket of the cigarette, and in the process allowed my cigarette to fall down on the floor.

I bent down to pick it up and very cautiously, brought out the object that was handed to me by Greg. I did my job as smart and as fast as I could as though nothing happened. I was in time to see the chauffeur of another car close by come out of his Jaguar and said, "Gee, what's going on. What do you have under that car?" He was a short, thickset, and unfriendly-looking man.

"Hey, my friend, how're you doing? I've got a loose breath already. Jerry's performing great out there. Why are you god damned not watching?" I was all the while smiling, but my heart was hammering as I walked towards him.

He smiled and shrugged. "We can hear the music from here, anyway… But l want to smoke now. Do you have a stick for me?"

"Oh, yes, you get it right away." I handed him the full packet. He peeled out four sticks. "I just smashed my goggles now," I told him calmly.

As he lit his cigarette stick, he gave me a friendly pat on my shoulder and said, "Sorry pal, sorry. Thank you for the sticks." He moved back towards the Jaguar.

"So long…." I moved over towards the chauffeur of Jerry's Rolls Royce. His head was resting on the steering and the driver's door was ajar and some soft music bleating off.

I thumbed his back, he raised his head, looked at me, and leaned back into the leather seat of the Rolls. He looked at me with wild eyes the way a tiger would look at a hyena. I smiled softly, but he didn't respond. "What's it?" he asked.

"I can see you are very lonely. You couldn't even reach out and have a snack or two and some ice cream?" I reached out my hand for a handshake. "I'm Harrison, Special Agent, Federal Bureau of investigation- FBI."

He forced a grin, but it didn't come out. He gripped my hand and shook it. "I'm Paul Doves, Jerry Martins' chauffeur." He had a cracked voice. He was a white man and about forty.

I offered my packet of cigarettes. He picked a stick and dangled it in between his lips. He asked for a lighter. I gave him one. He lit it. "This Martins' is a wonderful performer. He is performing wonders on stage. I just came out to buy myself ice cream and a cigarette. I quickly decided to take a stroll."

"Yeah, I agree with you. He's my buddy any day, yo."

We smoked together for a while, talked briefly as though we'd known ourselves for a while, and then embraced him and left. I was just acting. He would never be aware l had a mission. "See you some other time, my friend," I said.

"Thanks for the cig."

I walked back to the concert theater. A bunch of pretty young girls were almost bursting at their seams flapping and jumping up and grinning excitedly. Jerry Martins was performing excellently on stage. I gradually fell in love with this young singer. The urge was getting stronger to quit the deal. An hour and a half later, towards the end of the concert, I left my position again and walked back to the large entrance. I bought a small bottle of gin, ripped the cork open, and gulped it down. I strolled towards the parking lot. I noticed that all the chauffeurs of the vehicles that came with Jerry Martins were already on the wheels. When I got to his Rolls, I systematically stole a quick glance at where I had fixed the small object, the black destroyer. A chilly sensation ran down my spines, as the object was no longer there. *Something is mischievous here*, something *is mysterious here*, my thoughts kept banging. *I could have been spotted placing the object under the wheel of the Rolls Royce. I never trusted that dude I offered cigarettes, anyway.*

As I wiped my face of the sudden sweat that had blinded me, I raised my head up, looked down towards the direction of the concert, and noticed two cops pointing their fingers towards my direction.

I froze for a while but comforted myself as quickly as l could. Ten minutes later, six bodyguards led Jerry Martins towards his Rolls Royce. And minutes later, he was driven away in a long motorcade. I and the rest of my team assembled as fast as possible. We got into our Rolls Royce and the second car and smartly drove behind the motorcade of J-Martins. Our second car, a Buick truck had a police sticker, siren, and flashlight at the roof of the car – all licensed. There was no room for suspicion as we trailed his motorcade. Gregory Hill was unavoidably unhappy. The whole plot seemed to have failed! "Keep a tag behind him, Jim," he told Jim Hadley who was on the wheels. He was drinking straight from the bottle of Cognac.

I returned Rita's missed calls. She told me she was at the concert. I was shocked because she never told me she had the intention of sneaking in. "I was just watching your back. I don't trust these guys you're working for."

"Thanks, darling."

It was nudging 21.15 hours. I was able to catch the 21:21 hours express train back to New York.

# CHAPTER 5

I got into the hotel lobby basement through the revolving door. I asked the waiter to serve me a glass of Hennessy-on-the-rocks. I was in the lobby for about an hour before riding the elevator to the floor where I was lodged. It looked as if my room was searched, but by whom? I thought about that for a while but shaved off the thought. The next morning I shaved, took a bath, and dressed up. I packed up my suitcase and rode the elevator to the lobby on the basement floor for breakfast, before lodging out.

Shortly after, I passed through the thick-paneled revolving electronic door and headed to my car, the Buick, where it was parked in the bay. I inserted the key in the ignition, turned it for the second time before the engine woke up from slumber. I drove out of the bay into the long drive. At the gate, I handed back my parking card to the security man. I had noticed for some time that l had been run over by a black Lincoln – but I never took that seriously until today when l drove to a grocery shop to purchase a few items, after which l drove to "Jelly J. Bar." I had arranged with Greg Hills that l could be picked up at Jelly J. Bar, that I would be there briefly at noon for pizza.

A few minutes later as I was chewing my pizza, Nixon appeared. I asked him to take a seat. I ordered some sandwiches for him as that was his favorite.
"Sorry, I was late," he said, smiling. He was a cool, gentle chap. He was always indulged in reading magazines and playing scrabbles in his spare time. He was of average height, had lovely eyes, and always wore a full beard. He was a black American.

I grinned and shrugged. "No qualms, bro."

We discussed at length in general terms – how we lost in the last operation, our failures, and the critical way forward. A quarter of an hour later we were on our way.
We drove off in our different cars. After thirty minutes' drive back to New York City, I noticed through the rearview mirror the same black Lincoln coming fifty yards behind me. But who could this be? I noticed my hands trembling slightly on the wheel. Should l tell Nixon about this? Would he ever tell me the truth if for any reason he was aware? I drove behind Nixon. He knew the way better than me. We finally drove down through a driveway that overlooked a fine bungalow with a white tiled roof and chalky white wall. As we drove into the promenade, I didn't notice Lincoln tailing me anymore. Nixon Adams opened the verandah door and we carried the luggage into a compactly furnished lounging room. I flung my suitcase on an

armchair and said, "This place is cute."

"Yeah," he concurred.

I opened the door in front of me and saw myself in a small cocktail bar. "Suit yourself, Max. Oh, Sorry, Dick." We combed the apartment together, admiring the comfort. A few minutes later he said, "l must leave you now. Everything you want is in this house. Enjoy yourself."

I shook hands with him, while he patted me on my shoulder. "Thank you so much, Nix. See you soon." He left and shut the door behind him. As l probed further, I discovered a small cocktail bar by my left. I poured myself half-pint of Cognac. I looked to my left and saw a single cabinet bed whose sheets were folded normally and kept on top of the pillow. I noticed the wardrobe, the telephone sitting on the bedside table, the dressing mirror, a desk, and an upright chair opposite the desk. The dressing mirror stood gallantly in the middle of C-shaped furniture bearing four drawers with their keys hung out.

I opened the shelves one after the other. The second one contained a writing pad, a bunch of envelopes, and a pen-knife. The pen-knife was the only thing that caught my attention. I lifted it up, wondering what it could be doing there. As I took a closer look at it, my eyes went straight to the mirror and caught the image of a huge, tough, tight-faced man standing at the doorway just about a few meters away from me. He was pointing a gun at me.

My blood seemed to freeze. My heart began to thump. One thought came to my mind immediately. *This could be the guy tailing me ever since.* I pretended I hadn't seen him. I gradually balanced the pen-knife in my hand in case of a fight. "Take your hands up and don't move!" His voice was quite unfamiliar and threatening.

With that pretended shock, I turned suddenly and with all my strength thrust the dagger at him, aimed at his belly, and at the same time lurched to one side of the room in case of a shot. I heard the sound of a gunshot at the same time. The slug missed me, denting a permanent hole in the drawer. The dagger cut through his left arm. He released a second shot, this time not well positioned. The slug battered the mirror.

I rolled up from the floor as fast as possible towards his heels and shoveled his legs off the floor and that sent him thundering down with the force that almost shook the building. The gun fell off from his hand onto the floor near the doorway. He was now already in a pool of his blood. He stood up, advanced towards me, and gave me the hardest punch of my life in my belly. I fell off balance shortly. The sight of another lanky guy who came in through the same door holding a .25 Beretta got me awakened. He picked the .38 pistol lying on the doorway and tucked it into his hip pocket and hurriedly gave me a hard kick at my back on getting to me. "I am known as 'Di-Dude.' Now l want your hands up and don't make any silly move. My colleague is known as Otis Mafioso. You're under arrest for several charges. Now move." He pointed his gun at me, threatening at the same time. He motioned me to move out through the entrance door.

As the other first intruder struggled in pain and blood spilled, he said, "You're sunk for this act. I'll make sure you rot in jail."

Otis and I got onto the back seat of the Lincoln and Di-Dude got under the wheels. He screeched off the car from the bay and thundered down the promenade the way Hollywood actors would do. He pressed hard at the brakes when he got to the end of the driveway before accelerating hard in furtherance as though he was insane. "Where are you taking me to? Who are you guys? I was very nervous and uncomfortable. I glanced at the speedometer and discovered he was beating the stipulated speed limit of the area. About 20 yards ahead, I noticed a speed cop vehicle. De –Dude lowered his speed.

We finally drove into a compound with six other cars. We came from the car and they walked me down the short walkway towards a door. The inscription I saw at the door panel sent my blood racing: *New York Bad Boys.*
It was not surprising that the building was isolated.

Di-Dude opened the door. As we got inside the dim-lit hall, the deep smell of Indian hemp including others l could not comprehend, welcomed me and that made me sick. I began to cough. The hall was large and mercury-glowed. It had six long benches at different spots. On a fairly large table lay a glass ash-tray. There was nothing else in the hall other than three tall fellas whose eyes glittered red like the solemn setting sun. Otis Mafioso joined one of the three guys and they whispered to each other before leaving. "So, this is the handsome creep, ha?" asked one of them in between grins.

"Yeah…" replied Di-Dude, "he wanted to shake the life out of our Jerry Martins." He pointed at me: "Please take a seat, take a seat over there."

One of the men l met there poured whiskey into a glass and splashed it on my face. I yelled. He walked back and lit another Indian hemp to smoke. Another taller guy advanced, punching my head from three-time from behind. I collapsed on the floor. "Can somebody tell me what's going on here, before I call the police!" I screamed.

Another muscular guy said something callously: "Jerry Martins' our man. We're his private security operatives. We work behind the scenes. Call us the New York Bad Boys Org - NBBO. We watch his back from a distance. There's nothing that happens around him, behind him, in front of him, without our knowledge. When he goes around….we come around…you see. And you've fallen a victim. You were found trying to puncture his tires…the Rolls…remember? Think you're just an amateur- you're not smart enough." He giggled.

That assertion got my heart pounding. *How did they know about it*? I thought. For the first time, I thought about Hills, Jim, and James. How would they know where I am right now?

"My name is Ho-Chianti. I want to teach you some lessons." He was holding an automatic shotgun. "Move close to the wall and take your hands up." He came close to me, searched, and disarmed me – he found my pistol in the inner pocket of my jacket. He took my wallet and iPhone as well. "Count from 1 to 6. When you get to six, then you can say your last prayer."

I couldn't explain how l felt, but l knew my soul had already flown out of me because l was emotionally dead and motionless. I heard him bark again, "Now count!!

"You're accusing me of something I didn't do. How dare you say I tried to puncture the tire of the Rolls Royce. I can hardly fathom what you were talking about…." I couldn't finish my statement before he barked again:

"Count from 1 to 6!"

"One, two, three," I was taking it very slowly, but with some elasticity and hesitation. "Four.... Five...." Before I completed 'five' I heard the door burst open. With that sudden and unexpected break-in, we all turned to look behind us.

Behold, who I saw at the doorway pointing double SMGs towards our direction, baffled me. *How did Jim Harley and James Coins locate me? These guys are something else,* I thought. That revealed to me that they were also trailing me anywhere l went – anyhow!

They were ready to shoot...and ready to kill! For a few seconds, l tried to suck in some air, air of freshness and relief. I noticed Ho-Chianti was about to cock his gun to fire. I reacted as fast as I could: I knocked the gun out of his hand, sprinted and caught the gun on the floor, raised it up in readiness to fire. Twins and Harley had covered up the other two people. "Were police detectives," announced James. "Take your hands up, put down your guns. Now!"

I had this slight opportunity to run out of the hall towards the car park. I ran down the promenade, then into the avenue. Four hundred meters down the belly of the avenue, I stopped and leaned against a palm frond, breathing heavily. I waited patiently for Harley and James to join me. I kept wondering how they discovered where the NBBO had taken them. *Smart guys*! About five minutes later l saw their car down the avenue driving slowly towards my direction, most probably searching for where l was. I stepped out of the spot l was and walked to the middle of the road and waved both hands continuously.

I saw that the car accelerated immediately when they saw me. "Please hop inside the car," said Jim Harley.

I jumped into the back seat of the opened back door of the Range Rover and James drove off. "How did you guys handle them?" I asked.

"We locked them up in a room there," James said, as he drove briskly and smartly out of the deadly, but quiet zone.

"Thanks, great for saving my life, guys. Meanwhile, please take me to any pharmacy, James, let me take some treatment. You guys can leave me there. I will take a taxi to the airport and fly back later to Philadelphia. These guys beat me to a pulp."

"No qualms," James concurred, without any slight hesitation. James dropped me at a popular pharmacy along the way and drove off. I was treated for the bruises on my nose and neck. I bought some drugs and other kits. I walked into a phone booth by the corner and made a call to Greg Hills to tell him about my unexpected experience and how l was saved by J and J.

"I'm aware," he said. "We're always on top of the game, Max. We're watching your back as well...for your safety! Hope you were not badly hurt?'

"I'm as sick as a dog, as I speak."

"Yeah, I know those creeps," said Hills. "I'll handle them. But you need to take two days off to take good care of yourself. Your phone and weapon will be replaced tomorrow. You might need to change from that location, or we provide you with some soft security."

"That'd be nice," I concurred. I noticed through the glass door that a young lady was standing in front of the telephone booth to make a call. Her figure was a 'take away'! Strong sex appeal! Jeez. But I swallowed some saliva as though I didn't see anything. *Men!*

"My first son's marking his birthday tomorrow. If you feel like partying tomorrow, you can come around. I'll send the venue of the party to you on WhatsApp if you don't mind….that's if you're fit enough to come over."

"That'd be pretty great, sir."

"Ok, bye, and please take good care of yourself."

Slowly, I dropped the receiver, glared at my wristwatch. The evening was fast aging. As the young lady saw I was about to open the door, she stepped backward. I stepped out of the phone booth, then gave her a wide, toothy smile. "What a figure you've got! You could wake a sleeping corpse with your shape, pretty."

She smiled and said, "Thanks. You're handsome too. You took a while there…you were probably talking to your babe?" She looked friendly though. She wore apple brunette hair that extended down to the back of her waist. Her eyes were small, sea blue and the bone structure of her face was impressively the shape of an egg. Her breasts were as impressively shaped and pointed as the early August moon. She was wearing skin-tight jeans trousers that took her shape. She had on her small handbag across her shoulder. The fragrance of her perfume, the tone of her voice, and her physique made me almost breathless.

"You got it, babe. That chick of mine is troublesome. She was telling me that singer Jerry Martins performed brilliantly recently."

"Yeah," she grinned. "Jerry is a man I so cherish… my favorite American singer for now. What's your opinion about him?"

"He's a young man of spick and span. A handsome, multi-talented singer endowed especially by God. He's an epitome of love songs," I concluded, smiling. "Thank you. He has such qualities," she said.

We were gradually developing a rapport. One of the chances of getting a lady is if she gives an ear to talk to. It gradually dawned on me that she was the specimen l had been looking for to do this job for me. J-Martins would love her when he saw her. I was also yet to find out if Jerry was a womanizer. All singers are all womanizers as it were. They don't even need to hunt for them, the women scramble over themselves to catch a date with them. She could be God sent. "It seems you've dined with JM, the way you talk," I said, all smiles.

"Hey, you. He's my pal. He screws me, right. Let me make this important call, please." She got into the 'phone booth' and shut the door.

I walked three steps away and paused, remaining rooted on my track when I noticed Di-Dude move into the Juke-box with a fine blond chick about 20 yards in front of me. I was sure he didn't see me. Five minutes later, the young lady came out from the telephone booth. She cat-walked towards a red, sleek Porsche, opened the driver's door, and sat down. She waved at me to join her, as she noticed I was watching her, quite undecided. "Please come right in," she said. I opened the door and sat on the passenger's seat next to her. "My name is Cynthia, Cynthia Brentwood. I know you like me, the way you've been staring at me. I always tell people to go for what they like or admire. If you like a *brod,* go for her…except she's hooked. Enjoy life, life's too short."

It took me a few seconds to readjust from my shock. What a mature lady's talk. She swept me off my feet! So wild? "Call me Max," I said.

"Nice meeting you, Max. That's a fine name. You're very handsome." She inserted the key in the ignition and turned it. The car's interior was very cozy and smelt really good – the perfume she wore in combination with the air freshener in the car. The yellow interior of the car added so much panache to it.

"It's my pleasure."

"So, where're you headed?" She asked me.

"I was actually heading to the airport. I had a breakdown. My car has been towed away by the mechanic," I lied.

"I can drop you off where you can get an Uber or taxi; 'I am in a bit of a hurry," she said.

"Can we go for a drink downtown? I'm free this evening. We can hang out….l like movies….feel me?"

"I've got a date tonight, my dear. We can do dinner some other time." Even as she looked as ageless as the sun, there was something about her that refused to click in my brain fast enough. Could she be an informant, a mere socialite, or something?

Ladies in this particular trade line work differently, and perfectly too: they don't wait for you to 'ask them out,' they 'ask you out! With spy-catchers, it could be worse. They're like worms charmed by the mermaids: beautiful with strong magnetic sex appeal that you can hardly resist. When you get into their nets, you go down with them, you're done for … when actually you're their target.

She dropped me at the next taxi stand. We exchanged telephone numbers. In addition, she offered me her complimentary card. The card indicated that she was the owner of a firm of legal practitioners. "Let's talk on the phone tomorrow? I've got a job for you, a job worth some good bucks."

She was surprised. "A job worth some good bucks?" She stared briefly at me. "I like to do deals. I'm a property as well as a civil lawyer. Am a real estate guru as it were."

"I think we can flow? Let's flow then." I whispered to her, all smiles. I winked at her as I alighted from the car.

"Will expect your call tomorrow by noon, ok."

# CHAPTER 6

I joined Greg and Nixon at the dining. There was a covered plate at the other end of the table. Greg pointed his finger towards the covered plate. I sat down and joined them in the breakfast menu. "How're you doing? I do hope the pain has been suppressed, Max?" Greg asked, not looking up.

"Somehow, since I swallowed some laxative," I said.

"You see, it is not easy to make money," Greg continued. '' meanwhile James will take you to your new house, a bungalow, immediately after this meeting."

"Sorry about that encounter," said Nixon. "I noticed some tail when we were driving… but I couldn't make anything out of it."

I nodded and shrugged. After we finished eating we all moved over to the sitting room. Gregory turned on the radio and the music that filtered in was that of Jerry Martins. The presenter announced innocently in his slanged American voice, "Our young artist Jerry Martins is now ruling not only the United States but the whole world, with his new album which is only 4 months old. The latest 'single' he dropped has sold seven million copies in the US, two million copies in Europe, and ninety thousand copies in Africa. He had a concert at Chamberlain Volts Square in Philadelphia a few days ago. Enjoy the music..." I sighed a sigh of relief. My mind flashed to the conclusion that J- Martins was the 'bomb' of the season. Three of us exchanged glances. Gregory Hills stood up. The radio presenter continued his commentary shortly after: "Our handsome doctor of music will be touring London in two months' time..." Greg switched off the radio with annoyance. "This son of a bitch!"

Nixon glanced at me; I returned the glance and he scowled. There was a short silence. "Max," he called me, looking directly into my eyes, "we've made some findings. J-M leaves his house every nine o'clock in the morning, except Sundays, to play golf in a millionaire friend's compound. This time, he doesn't drive in his Rolls Royce but a Mercedes Concord." He paused and lit a cigar. "It's about a fifteen minutes normal drive from his house to this millionaire friend's house. This time, he usually drove himself and without any bodyguard....maybe only two of them were sitting with him in the car. But don't mistake the fact that there could be a probability of a blue Pajero truck driving from behind. In this jeep could be two or three well-trained bodyguards on mufti." He tipped off some ash from the cigar into an ashtray after dragging in a long haul.

"What about those deadly dudes that kidnapped me days back? I'm scared of them. I would've been dead as we speak. They are like the devil, looking for whom to devour. They can appear from nowhere."

"Max, I already told you I'll handle those guys. I know all the good, the bad, and the ugly in New York, Chicago, and Philadelphia – these are where we've our branch offices. These are mine zones. Let me remind you: I'm the founder of this firm that has hired you; we're seasoned, refined, and organized. I call the shots here, ok. We don't take up any contract of fewer than 10 mils. We do clean and dirty 'contracts' as long as the money is huge. I'm close to all the cops and mafia kingpins in town. We cover 'covert' and 'overt' operations, depending on the direction of the music. We've been involved in deadlier and trickier contracts than this. For those creeps that messed you up, I'm in the process of sealing up their career. Leave that to me." He paused and tipped off another ash from his cigar.

I nodded. He continued: "The name of this billionaire is Kent Daniels, six-footer, heavily built, handsome, and a blonde. He's about forty-five. He's J-Martins' confidant and like a father to him. One of his police orderlies is my friend. I will call him later, to tell him that I want to witness the next friendly golf match where J-Martins would be present. As few as ten of his fans are allowed in the compound to watch the game at any point in time. At least ten armed policemen are present in this compound 24 hours a day. That's what we'll do, Max: I'll go there with you. Try to familiarize yourself with him. After the game and our gentlemen want to leave, you tell him to give you a lift. Before the end of the golf game, you must've talked jovially with him, developing a fast rapport with him, if you're smart. Compliment him very well for his excellent performance at his last concert and all his music. He likes compliments and he likes young women very much. Just warm into his heart. He's not a snub...very nice guy as it were. If he agrees to give you a ride, attempt to present him with the small perfume... as we had earlier planned..." he paused, snuffed life out of the cigar, took another stick, and lit it. He was a chain smoker. He paused for a while to drag in the scented smoke from his cigar. "Housed in Kent Daniels´ ranch are table-tennis, badminton, and lawn tennis courts and a mini-golf course. His compound is more of a mini ranch. About six of his close billionaire allies, including Jerry Martins, an ex-governor of New York, come around to play golf and tennis almost every other weekend."

"Golf's the game of the rich and the pot bellied rich men," I said, smiling, just trying to create fun.

"Even our president plays golf," said Nixon.

His telephone rang. He picked it up, then stood up. "Greg here. Hello?" He started pacing the room. "Oh, Meg, Sorry. Yeah. I'll do that. I'm actually in a meeting now, ok. No, I've not forgotten, I know the time of your flight. Or has it changed?" He paused briefly, then replied on the phone, "Ok, on my way now to the airport. See you soon. My wife's just phoned, l need to pick her up. This meeting has ended. I will call for another meeting tomorrow evening."

# CHAPTER 7

When I got to my new bungalow in New York, which Greg had made available about a week ago, I saw a Porsche parked by the side of the house. There were only three parking ports by the side of the bungalow. The Porsche was exactly like that driven by Cynthia Brentwood. *What is her car doing here? Where could she be now? Is she probably in the bungalow? Who gave her my keys!* My thoughts were loud.

I parked my car by the side of the Porsche, alighted, walked to the door, and turned the knob slightly. It was not locked. I pushed the door in and stood there for a while, surveying the whole place, waiting also to hear a sound - any sound.
There was no sound, other than that of the ticking clock placed on the mantelpiece.

I walked in as stealthily as a cat, then shut the door slightly. I was cautiously nervous. I tiptoed towards the door leading into my bedroom, slightly turned the knob, and then opened the door cautiously. What I saw made my heart seize for a while. Lying on the bed, naked, but only in red panties with a matching pair of brassiere, with both legs spread apart, cigarette dangling between her lips, reading a novel, was the exact lady whose thought had come to my mind immediately when I saw the Porsche. That was Cynthia Brentwood – the movie star and a professional lawyer, from what she told me. *Is she also a porn star?* I thought. At that sight, any unstable man would jump into that bed and begin to screw her.

The beauty of her body was indescribable! She looked at me and smiled. I didn't smile back for I was not happy about this action. I was not expecting her. We only had dinner once, at which point I gave her my address. My heartbeat was reassuring. I was in a good time to feel the upward movement of my third leg as it pressed hard against my trousers more anxious than l had thought. Her pair of breasts were wonderful - they were like a pair of overripe pawpaw. I held my urge sternly. The Satan part of my mind told me to jump on her. This one could send one to prison - for rape or attempted rape, what so many American women are known for - to bring down powerful men. Screwing this type, one has to be careful – you have to be invited to the dining table! I remember she told me she was a lawyer, as well as a film star - a rare career combination. She appeared more like a 'sex queen,' 'devil diamond,' than a professional lawyer, a professional real estate guru. She could thrive better as a detective, as a spy-catcher working for the security agencies. *Hey, Max, be careful,* one mind whispered to me. My thoughts were pretty organic.

"How did you get in here? I was not actually expecting you, right?" I asked her. I was calm now.

"Weren't you the one that dropped the keys under the foot mat at the doorpost? That's where I picked it up."

I peered at her deeply. She was right. "But how did you find out I keep my keys there?"

"My instincts."

*What a wonderful brod!* I thought. *This's just another bad girl! Should I bring her into the 'bloody contract'?* I sat beside her on the bed. "Oh yeah, I guess you could come around anytime. But l was not expecting you."

"Please don't talk too much. Join me in bed. I've not been feeling well since I met you. The mere thought of you, your sex appeal, makes me wet continuously. Please come and give it to me. I'm fully wet down there."

"Please give me a minute." My 'third leg' got harder and wanted to jump out of my pants. *Are there better devils than 'some' women and their bodies? Some are just mermaids! Christ!* I flung my pants away and joined her in bed. She was probably not shocked seeing how large my 'third leg' was. There was no time for foreplay. Short kisses here and there; use of my fingers. That spot was completely wet. She was honest about that. She was screaming all the while screaming. Ecstasy. Body magnets. Magnetic grips. Aromatic feelings. When l penetrated, I didn't last two minutes before l arrived. *Gadem!*

It was 3:00 AM. We could have been in that bed for more than six hours, making love, falling asleep, waking up again, and having further rounds of sex. I discovered on the floor that the bottle of Vat 69 was almost empty. Both of us had been gulping down excess liquor.

We moved over to the lounge. She went into the kitchen shortly and returned shortly with coffee for two. She wore just her red, sexy pants and brassiere and was stepping on a pair of moccasins that she brought with her. I was in my boxer shorts. I sipped from my cup of coffee, walked to the bar, picked another bottle of Vat 69, opened it, and poured some in my coffee. She lit a stick of cigar. From her seeming way of life it was obvious, she was a '*hard girl*' who had been on the street. Wild girl, you can say that again and again. As she smoked her cigar, she added some Indian hemp to her coffee.

"Let's do a deal, Cynthia. I'll give you two million bucks if you can pull this contract through. I do hope l can confide in you?"

"I'm all ears. I was once a street girl. I can pull any

deal...even if I need to fuck the president to pull the strings, I'll do it, as far as the pay is fat."

I sighed. "I'm doing a contract for an organization. I might need your help. You're like God sent."

"I'm listening. Go straight to the point, Max." She puffed smoke towards my face.

"They want Jerry Martins kidnapped.....without any trace. What they'll do with him after then, is none of my business." I paused, stared at her, and saw a change of expression on her face. She was silent for a while, deep in thought, but nodding continuously.

"It's not a problem. What's the total package?"

"USD$3.5 mil," I lied.

"I take 40 percent, you take 60. I get 1.5, you get 2 mils."

"Not acceptable. You get one million."

"No deal," she said, sipping on her drink.

"Question is, have you got the guts to do the job?"

"I just need one week. I'm a beautiful woman. I'll look for him anywhere....I'll fuck him and the rest... leave the rest for me. All male singers/artists love women; J-M is not an exception."

"Deal. You'll get the 40 percent," I said. For another

ten minutes, l briefed her on what we needed to do for a successful operation, leaving no stone unturned.

"Let me ask you some personal questions."

"'Am all ears, honey."

"You look rich…your appearance, your perfume, your car, your lifestyle. Talk to me," I said smiling. "You amaze me…you carry some charm…some panache. I think I'm falling for you. Sex with you wao!" I meant every word I said.

She stood up and started pacing the room. "For any movie l feature, I earn a million dollars. If 'am playing a lead role, l make 2 mils. It doesn't come all the time –maybe once every two or three years. I make money from property sales –land and houses. I buy, renovate and resell properties. I don't go to court, am just a property buy and sell lawyer…but if you offend me I'll put you behind bars." We laughed hilariously. My problem is… I am a spendthrift. I take the white one, you know what l mean. I've got a special cigar brand from Italy. I bought myself a big mansion on the hills of Manhattan….a mansion quite bigger than the owner. When you see it you'll think I am a millionaire. But I am only a hustler. You see, all these cost money. I love comfort. I live comfortably, at all cost.``

"I understand what you mean, C-Y."

"I need an advance payment before 1 can do anything," she said.

I smiled. "How much?"

"Half payment. You balance up when the deal is complete," she concluded.

"Please send your account number to me via my WhatsApp."

# CHAPTER 8

I joined Rita Shores for dinner on Saturday – a day after l sealed the deal with Cynthia. I had had several missed calls from Janet but had not the slightest urge to return her calls and messages. When l did call her after l dispatched Cynthia, she was at first angry and worried not to have heard from me – as she told me she was always 'watching my back,' against the backdrop of the *Bloody Contract* l was engaged in and the crop of people behind the contract. "Please let's have dinner tomorrow evening – Saturday. Pack your bag to stay here for the entire weekend. And sharpen your *third leg* very well, because I've not had sex for a while." That conversation alone suddenly awakened my third leg. *Women! Mini Satan! Mermaids. They know how to get it from you. You can hardly resist it like a man (75 percent, pro); when they don't want it, they can handle it; when you force them, it becomes rape, and the law will come for you as soon as she reports the case. This has run so many wealthy and powerful men aground in the States.* My thoughts were loud in my mind with anger.

I gave in. I needed her for so many reasons: she

was watching my back because she never trusted Gregory Hills and his team (That l thought, was out of love); she was very beautiful, from very rich parents who would be bequeathing their wealth to her as an only daughter (it was just for me to match the love she already had for me and I would propose to her because I already foresaw the commitment chemistry); her good heart and the spirit to assist a man like me. Not so many rich ladies want to lift a man up. If they are rich, most of them still want their own money, even if they have to strangle you financially. But if you are lucky to meet these few kind ones with good hearts, keep them forever by marrying them, for they're rare gems. Above all, she was already running a personal and quite lucrative business.

I spent the entire weekend with Rita. It was one of the most memorable weekends l would have had for a very long time. I had always reasoned that when a woman needs you, she will get you mainly through the magnetic powers God gave to them: good and exhaustive sex, excessive and very nice food, being extremely nice, and zero nagging modes! All men would fall for these charms. Alas, after she had got you in her trap, she might on a 40 percent basis overturn her character sometime in the future. Character trait! That's a conversation for another day. But they are the central nervous systems (CNS) of all men.

Monday morning. It was 9.00 hours when I drove off from Janet's residence after a full-blown and quite lovely weekend with her and headed to Kent Daniel's residence. Gregory's description of the ranch was very accurate. The ranch was palatial and many sports outfits fitted in quite comfortably.
I was able to drive in through the huge gate entrance after a short interrogation by the security man that came out of his tent to talk to me. Greg had told me he would do his homework before l got there.

I drove down the 200-meter-long whistling-pine-lined promenade towards a small house sitting at the edge of the mini-golf club. I parked the Buick in between a Packard Clipper and a Mercury, in a well-ventilated Pavilion. I stepped down, locked the car, and was admiring Mercury when a voice said, "It costs only a hundred thousand dollars..."

I was wondering who owned that voice. I turned, then saw him walking towards me. From his appearance and carriage, I didn't doubt the fact that he was Kent Daniels. I had seen him several times on television. He was a tall, handsome white American. His face and head were bare – cleanly shaven! His frame was athletic and trim, far from being muscular, but appeared very sharp and smart for his age of about sixty. He was smartly dressed in sneakers, tracksuit, and fez-cap, all white. "The car is for the super-rich," I said, smiling.

I shook hands with him. "I'm Robert, one of J-Martins' bodyguards."

"He comes here often, but your face is not familiar."

"We work behind the scenes for his protection, sir," I lied again. "Am in the team that combs the place he needs to visit before he takes off. I'm on a short vacation."

"Nice. I'm Kent. Am the gardener here," he said, smiling.

I laughed out loud. "You can say that again. Who doesn't know Kent Daniels, the famous music producer, and director, the multimillionaire, the father of numerous musical artists in the United States....the God-father of my boss, J-Martins." Fifty yards ahead of where l was standing, l noticed two teenage girls playing badminton. They were dressed in resplendent white sneakers, white tracksuits, and white fez-Cap.

"I'm sure you're for some warm-ups," he said, smiling.

I had never met such a humble man with a very simple appearance. He was actually clutching a long flower cutter, to demonstrate that he was actually trimming the flowers a while ago, a man of his stature – very simple and humble. I'm just doing some gardening." He didn't even look like a multi-millionaire who owned a Mercury and a fleet of exclusive automobiles.

"Exactly. I want to see what l can do with my short vacation. But why do you do the gardening yourself, sir?"

"It's a form of exercise for me. I engage myself once in a while. I've got a gardener though." I noticed him as he looked me up from head to toe. "I like your outfit. Everything blue to match – your sneakers, polo, and trainer pants. Tiger Woods! I like Tiger Woods."

I smiled. I was honestly enjoying the company of such a man of a high statue, a crème-de-la-crème: that fact made having a tete-a-tete with him right now, more interesting for me.

Five days later Cynthia called me on the phone. She said she wanted to see me urgently - not at her residence, nor mine, but at the low-class *'Charity Tavern,'* a drinking bar a few kilometers west of downtown. When we got there, she ordered whisky on the rocks with lemon to garnish. I did the same. "You sound so worried. Is everything ok?" I asked her.

"Everything is not ok, but everything is ok for you and your team."

"You're talking in parables. Talk to me, please."

She leaned forward and whispered into my ears: "The operation was successful. I need my balance today. 'Am leaving town for the meantime. I've bought a one-way ticket to the Bahamas."

"Are you kidding me? It sounds easy…you don't mean the shit!?" I thought at first she was joking, but asking for her balance payment and saying she had already bought a ticket to the Bahamas, put paid to the statement.

"How exactly did you do it? Was it exactly the way we planned it?"

"What matters is that the job has been done, and successfully at that," she said. I noticed she was somewhat nervous.

I gulped my drink, poured again, and swallowed deeper. I instantly became nervous. Shortly after, the television mounted on the wall close by suddenly had a Breaking News headline. "A sad news has just hit The United States. Our dear musical artist multi-millionaire, Mr. Jerry Martins: 'J-Boy', has been poisoned by one of his girlfriends. He's in an emergency situation. No death has actually been confirmed." The full picture of Cynthia Brentwood was cast on the TV. "The last woman J-Boy reportedly saw was the picture displayed here. The name has not been confirmed as of press time. She's therefore declared wanted. Finger-prints operatives from the FBI and newsmen are storming his compound as of now…" said the newscaster, before switching to another headline.

For a few seconds, I stared deeply into her face. I heard her speak, but it came to me faintly: "Are you now convinced? Let's leave here now, Max. And l need my balance now, so I can leave town tonight."

"You're a professional: That was a neat job. But now, you're at risk of being caught by the cops. I too, because l know when you're caught, you're surely going to mention my name, right?"

"You just mentioned that I'm a professional and that means they'll not get me and I'll never mention your name at any cost….as far as you pay me my balance."

I gulped my drink and we sneaked out quietly into her car. I grabbed my phone as we sat down and dialed Gregory Hills immediately. I noticed Cynthia brought out a patchwork- face from underneath the seat she sat on and wore it neatly. She took out another blouse and exchanged it for the green one she was wearing. She was suddenly looking different now.

"Good day sir."

"How're you doing Max?" responded Gregory Hills.

"Have you heard the news, sir?"

"Yeah…that he's in a coma. He's not confirmed dead yet."

"Cynthia wants her balance sir. She's leaving town immediately. Her photo is all over the media, the television."

"I didn't hire Cynthia, you did. You can pay her off… you get your balance when we are able to convey the message to Vicenti that…….J-Martino *has passed on.*"

"That's outrageous, sir," I said, not very comfortable with the way the drama was suddenly playing out.

Cynthia grabbed the iPhone from me and started speaking with a stentorian voice: "Mr. Greg, I don't want any problem with you. Kindly transfer my balance in the next minute or l tell it to the president of the United States, or call the cops on you for your illegal deals."

I heard Gregory Hills laughing in the background. "I should be the one calling the FBI or the cops on you, not the other way round. It's your photograph on the TV, not mine. You should leave town immediately, no need to threaten anyone. You will get your payment as soon as the contract is fully delivered….you know what l mean."

She flanged my phone on my lap angrily. "You'll go in for this, Max. I'll be needing my money in the next

48 hours. I'll send my account details. Please get down from my car."

I quietly stepped down from her car and saw her screech off with tortured tires, as she joined the motorway.

*Is Gregory Hills up to some games?* That thought kept banging in my head. I hope he had not forgotten the 'two-week-long vacation with your spouse in the Bahamas after the contract,' a promise he earlier made to me? I hope Greg was not changing the entire narrative as earlier planned? The entire scenery was playing out like a betrayal! *The president really needs to hear about this, as Cynthia rightly said*, I thought.

# THE LAST CHAPTER

Gregory Hills and his team put Max on the front burner in the business to eliminate Jerry Martins. He was compelled against his will to carry out such a plan. When Max was done, Greg became the investigator with very vital evidence to nail Max. A double standard contract for double settlements?

'Huge Dogs Inc.,' was a double standard organization that was overtly 'above the surface,' but covertly underworld and ultimately deadly. Greg later found out that it was not Max that did the job, but Cynthia.

Rita was the only 'good girl.'

J-Martins didn't die eventually – by the grace of God. The court ruled that it was 'an attempted murder.' Cynthia went into thin air after the operation– she was never found!

Max had spent two years behind bars before his attorney unveiled, with the aid of the FBI, that the 'masked man' behind *'Bloody Contract'* was Gregory

Hills, the director of 'Huge Dogs Inc.' He was picked up after months of exhaustive tracking in Berne, Switzerland, by Interpol.

His double-faced and deceptive organization was shut down after a thorough investigation by the forensic department of the FBI.

Max reunited with Rita after he was released.

They tied the knot six months afterward. Few months after the marriage, Rita handed over full control and directorship of her estate and companies respectively, worth about USD$95m, which were bequeathed to her by her late parents as an only daughter, to her husband, Max.
The union was blessed with twins two years later - two boys.

This was what love could be like. They had since lived in harmony ever after in Long Beach, California, USA.

There are still some men and women with very good hearts.

# ABOUT THE AUTHOR

## Keem-Holems Ojei

Keem-Holems Ojei is a Nigerian-born German author, accountant, talent-hunt promoter and the publisher of KSD Digest 'NovZine.' He was a banker and had also worked as an accountant in an oil-servicing and construction company.
An alumnus of ESUT Business School, Enugu, Nigeria; VHS Schule, Bielefeld, Germany, etc,

Ojei has authored several books amongst which are: Nations In Chains, Priceless Jewel, 'Ogbanje' Twins And Other Stories, The Petrodollar Chieftains, The Narcodollar Chieftains and State Secret code-named, 'Beyond Salvage.' His hobbies remain writing, meeting, and advising people of all walks of life.